A WRINKLE IN TIME

by
Madeleine L'Engle

Teacher Guide

Written by
Anne Troy

Note

The Dell Yearling paperback edition of the book was used to prepare this guide. The page references may differ in the hardcover or other paperback editions.

Please note: Please assess the appropriateness of this book for the age level and maturity of your students prior to reading and discussing it with your class.

ISBN 1-56137-118-1

To order, contact your local school supply store, or—

Novel Units, Inc.
P.O. Box 433
Bulverde, TX 78163-0433

Web site: www.educyberstor.com

Table of Contents

Skills and Strategies

Thinking
Brainstorming, classifying and categorizing, evaluating, analyzing details, synthesizing ideas

Comprehension
Predicting, sequencing, cause and effect, inference, comparison/contrast

Listening/Speaking
Participation in discussion, drama

Literary Elements
Point of view, characterization, imagery, mood, plot, figurative language, conflict, suspense, dialogue, style

Vocabulary
Synonyms, antonyms, multiple meaning words, context, etymology of words

Writing
Dialogue, comparison, description, summary

Summary of *A Wrinkle in Time*

Charles Wallace Murry, a brilliant little boy, Meg Murry, his stubborn 12-year-old sister and Calvin O'Keefe, a 14-year-old friend, begin a search for their missing father, Mr. Murry, a government scientist. They are aided in their search by three women who have supernatural powers—Mrs. Whatsit, Mrs. Who, and Mrs. Which. To rescue Mr. Murry, the children travel by means of a wrinkle in time, or tesseract, to the evil planet of Camazotz. Charles is captured by the wicked people of Camazotz, and Meg must save her father and later Charles.

About the Author

Madeleine L'Engle is the author of more than forty books for children, receiving the Newbery Award Medal for *A Wrinkle in Time*. She lives in New York City and Goshen, Connecticut. She began writing when she was about five years old. "I always wanted to write, but I wasn't encouraged at home because my father was a writer…my early teachers didn't encourage me to write either." (Madeleine L'Engle, *The Irrational Season*, Seabury, 1977)

"School was something to be endured; I don't think I learned nearly as much from my formal education as from the books I read instead of doing homework, the daydreams, which took me on exciting adventures in which I was intrepid and fearless and graceful." (Madeleine L'Engle, *The Summer of the Great-Grandmother*, Farrar, 1974)

Madeleine L'Engle began her serious writing while she was in high school. She also had an active career in the theater.

Teacher Information

Science fiction and science fantasy are terms that are interchangeable for many students. They are likely to label "science fiction" for any book that includes the paraphernalia of science. Science fiction speculates on a world that might be possible, whereas fantasy presents a world that never was and never could be. Science fiction's aim is to suggest hypotheses about mankind's future or about the nature of the universe. Fantasies explain the way things might be in the real world or the way things should be. An important element of fantasy is the theme or special message. The author uses the imaginary world of fantasy to develop the theme.

A background in the theory of dimension is necessary for student understanding of this novel. Discuss and demonstrate the differences of the following:

- a) One dimensional—a straight line
- b) Two dimensional—a flat piece of paper
- c) Three dimensional—a cube, die, or box

Introductory Activities and Information

Note:

It is not intended that everything presented in this guide be done. Please be selective, and use discretion when choosing the activities you will do with the unit. The choices that are made should be appropriate for your use and your group of students. A wide range of activities has been provided so that individuals as well as groups may benefit.

1. Predictions: Have the students examine the cover illustration and the title. Ask what predictions they have about the book. Some prompts include: Does the picture on the cover give you any clues as to what this book is about? Who do you think the people on the cover are? What do you suppose happened right before—and right after—what is shown on the cover? What is the unusual creature? When and where do you think this novel takes place? What sort of story will this be? Funny? Sad? Adventure? Fantasy? Read the back cover of the book. How many of your questions are answered? What other questions come to your mind about the content of this book?

2. Anticipation Guide: Have students discuss whether they agree or disagree with the following statements—and why. Have them reconsider these statements after reading the novel.
    a) Parents can have problems too big for them to handle.
    b) Fantasy or make-believe stories are only for children.
    c) Brothers and sisters can really help one another.
    d) Very bright children may have problems with their peers.
    e) Sometimes it is better to keep silent about how you feel.
    f) You shouldn't worry about what other people say about you.

3. Prereading Discussion:

    Friendship: Think about adults who are your friends. What do you admire about them? What do they value? How have they helped you?

    Problem-Solving: What sorts of problems do you face? What steps do you take when you are faced with a problem? Is it easier to solve a problem by yourself or with a partner? Who is the best problem-solver you know? To whom would you go for help in solving a problem?

4. Log: Have students keep a response log as they read.

    *In one type of log, the student assumes the persona of one of the characters. Writing on one side of each piece of paper, the student writes in the first person ("I...") about his/her reactions to what happened in the chapter. A partner (or the teacher) responds to these writings on the other side of the paper, as if talking to the character.

    *In the dual entry log, students jot down brief summaries and reactions to each section of the novel they have read. (The first entry could be made based on a preview of the novel—a glance at the cover and a flip through the book.)

    *In the third type of log, students choose a passage from each section that strikes them for some reason, copy it, and explain why the passage seems important to them. (Has the author used language in a special way? Created amusing word pictures? Expressed an important insight? Reminded the student of something in his or her own life?)

    *Alternatively as students read, they might simply jot thoughts and questions on sticky notes and apply them to the passage in question for later reference during literature circle discussion.

5. Brainstorming: Write the word "tesseract" on the board. Have students suggest any ideas that come to mind when they hear the word, and jot these ideas around it. Help students "cluster" the ideas into categories. A sample framework is shown below. When the novel is completed, repeat this activity.

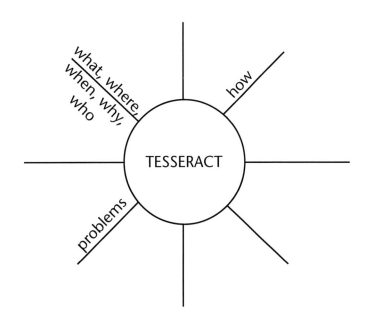

6. Writing: Have students freewrite for ten minutes using one of the following "starters."

- Two things people have to do for themselves...
- Brothers can be very different...
- Sometimes it is hard to be very smart...
- Courage means...
- Knowing who to trust is...

7. Instruct students to mark places with sticky notes with a **B** where Meg, Charles, and Calvin use their brains to solve problems and to mark places with an **L** where these characters have good luck. Students will refer back to these details when talking and writing about this novel. Have students put a star by parts of the story they found funny.

8. Story Diagram: Many novels have the same parts—a setting, a problem, a goal, and a series of events that lead to an ending or conclusion. These story elements may be placed on a diagram, which helps a reader to understand and to remember. (See page 10 of this guide.)

9. Develop a T-comparison chart. This is a science fiction/fantasy story which uses a shift in time to enable characters to enter an imaginary world.

Realistic Fiction	Fantasy/Science Fiction

Setting—our world
Characters—like us
	Setting—combination of real and
	     fantasy
	Characters—some characters like us
	     —talking animals
	     —characters with unusual powers

Action—could happen Problem—could be ours	—robots Action—never could happen Problem—unusual

Recommended Procedure:

This book may be used in several ways: a) read to the entire class; b) read with the class; or c) read in reading groups. It may be read one chapter at a time, using the DRTA, Directed Reading Thinking Activity Method. This technique involves reading a section, and then predicting what will happen next by making good guesses based on what has already occurred in the story. The predictions are recorded, and verified after subsequent reading has taken place. (See page 9 of this guide.)

Some Ideas for Vocabulary Study:
Note: The Novel Units® Student Packet for this title contains reproducible vocabulary activities.

1. Have the students map words, including several synonyms, an antonym if appropriate, some other forms of the word, a memory device or sketch to help them recall the definition, and/or some way to associate the word with their own experiences. The format can be left up to the students, or use a framework like the one below.

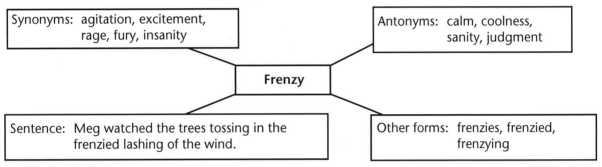

For a vocabulary list with many entries, make each student responsible for just one or two words. Display the maps, and give students ample opportunity to view them and make their own notes about words with which they are not familiar.

2. Have the students identify or generate synonyms of key words. For example, ask students to complete "synonym trains" for key words such as *pathetic*. (page 17)

    pathetic—pitiable—touching—moving—affecting—tender—plaintive

3. Context Clues: Students keep a log of important vocabulary words (selected either by them or by you), context clues (if any) and the definition for some, but not all of the words in the list. (Requiring students to look up every unfamiliar word is not advisable, as it can be an overwhelming task.) You might introduce this activity by mentioning a word in the story you didn't know and modeling your use of context and other clues to find the word's meaning. For example, "I didn't know what *raucous* (page 34) was. We learn from the words near *raucous* that it describes a crow's cry and the first syllable, *rauc*, reminds me of the word racket or noisy."

4. Have the students compose questions to ask classmates about the words. For example, a student might ask, "How would a belligerent student act?"

5. Divide the class into pairs and assign several words to each pair. After arriving at a simple definition for each of their assigned words, partners should create a mnemonic device to help them remember the definition. Definitions and mnemonics can be shared with the class.

6. Before they read a section, have students predict how the words on the vocabulary list will be used. For example, in Chapter 1, who might be *prodigious*? What might have be *relinquished*? Why is a *wraith-like* figure spooky?

7. As the students read, they select the 20 vocabulary words they feel it is most important to know to understand the story. Have them write one sentence for each word, explaining what the word has to do with the story.

8. Investigate the etymology of words on the list. Make semantic maps showing the root words and meanings and some other forms of the word.

Word: ANTAGONISTIC

- Root Word: antagonize
- Origin: Gk. antagonizesthai—to struggle against
- anti = against + agonizesthai + to struggle, strive
- Meanings: to make an enemy of; to struggle against; oppose; to counteract; neutralize
- Other forms of the word: antagonist
  antagonism
  antagonize
  antagonistic
  antagonistically

9. At the beginning of your study of *A Wrinkle in Time*, have students make separate pages in their notebooks with the headings "Emotion describers," "Place or Thing Describers," "Sensory Describers" (sound, taste, smell), and "People Describers." As students proceed with the reading, have them add words to the pages.

Using Predictions

We all make predictions as we read—little guesses about what will happen next, how the conflict will be resolved, which details given by the author will be important to the plot, which details will help to fill in our sense of a character. Students should be encouraged to predict, to make sensible guesses. As students work on predictions, these discussion questions can be used to guide them: What are some of the ways to predict? What is the process of a sophisticated reader's thinking and predicting? What clues does an author give us to help us in making our predictions? Why are some predictions more likely than others?

A predicting chart is for students to record their predictions. As each subsequent chapter is discussed, you can review and correct previous predictions. This procedure serves to focus on predictions and to review the stories.

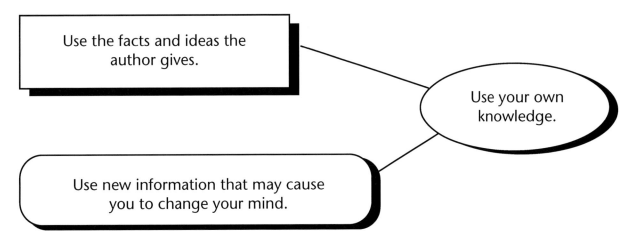

Prediction Chart

What characters have we met so far?	What is the conflict in the story?	What are your predictions?	Why did you make those predictions?

Story Map

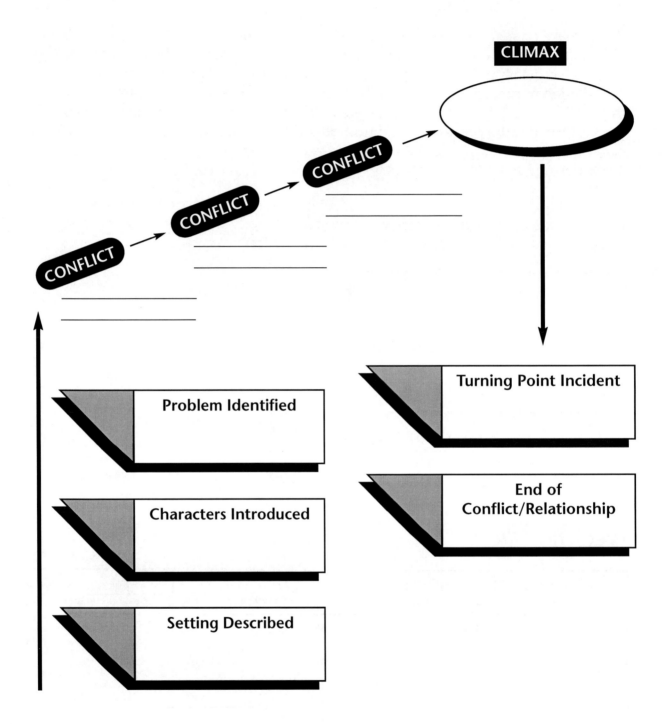

Using Character Webs

Attribute Webs are simply a visual representation of a character from the novel. They provide a systematic way for the students to organize and recap the information they have about a particular character. Attribute webs may be used after reading the novel to recapitulate information about a particular character or completed gradually as information unfolds, done individually, or finished as a group project.

One type of character attribute web uses these divisions:

- How a character acts and feels. (How does the character feel in this picture? How would you feel if this happened to you? How do you think the character feels?)

- How a character looks. (Close your eyes and picture the character. Describe him to me.)

- Where a character lives. (Where and when does the character live?)

- How others feel about the character. (How does another specific character feel about our character?)

In group discussion about the student attribute webs and specific characters, the teacher can ask for backup proof from the novel. You can also include inferential thinking.

Attribute webs need not be confined to characters. They may also be used to organize information about a concept, object or place.

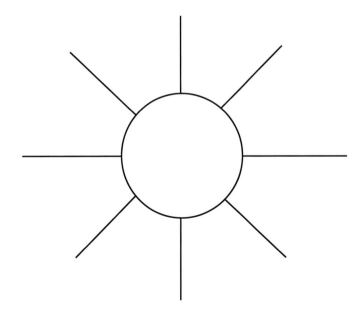

Attribute Web

The attribute web below will help you gather clues the author provides about a character in the novel. Fill in the blanks with words and phrases which tell how the character acts and looks, as well as what the character says and what others say about him or her.

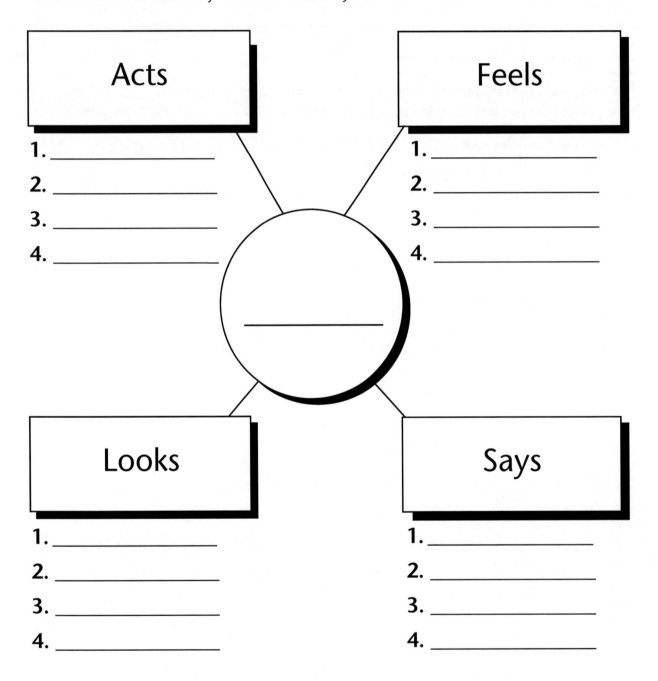

Chapter-by-Chapter Vocabulary, Discussion Questions, and Activities

Chapter 1: "Mrs. Whatsit"—Pages 3-21

Vocabulary:

frenzied 3	wraith-like 3	serenity 5	subsided 7
vulnerable 8	prodigious 11	repulsive 13	exclusive 13
indignantly 17	pathetic 17	vigorously 19	supine 20
agility 20	relinquished 20	frivoling 21	

Discussion Questions and Activities:

Predicting is very important in fantasy. Read only pages 3-4.

1. What do you learn about the characters? Where is the father? (*Characters— Meg or Margaret Murry, probably the protagonist, does not do well in school, fights when boys call her brother "dumb," has twin brothers; parents are supposedly brilliant; father has disappeared*)

2. Where does the story take place? (*not given on pages 3-4*)

3. What is the problem of the story? (*Page 4, Meg has many problems—with school, with teasing boys, etc. There also seems to be some problem related to Meg's father.*)

4. Let's begin a story diagram with the facts we have. We will add to it and change it as the story goes along. See page 10 of this guide.

5. Why do you think the chapter title is "Mrs. Whatsit"? Put your responses on the Prediction Chart.

Read pages 5-21

6. Why do you think Meg has problems? (*Father is gone. Charles Wallace is different. Mother is not like other mothers. The twins entertain one another and Meg is alone. Meg doesn't act like other girls in her class.*)

7. How is Charles Wallace different from other small boys? Begin an attribute web. After each chapter add to Charles' web.

8. What is "special" about Mrs. Murry? (*Pages 10-13, She's an understanding mother and she is beautiful.*)

9. What do we learn about Mrs. Whatsit? (*Page 14, Charles had met her when he rushed after the dog; she lives in an old house in the woods.*)

10. Why has Mrs. Whatsit come to visit? *(Page 17, In the storm she loses her way and is blown off course. She recognizes Charles Wallace's house by the smell.)*

11. What does Meg think of Mrs. Whatsit? What does Meg have against her? *(Page 17, Mrs. Whatsit wants Russian caviar, which the children are saving for Mother's birthday. Page 18, She barges into the house in the middle of the night; Meg does not think that Charles should have this kind of a friend; Mrs. Whatsit stole Mrs. Buncombe's sheets; Meg does not trust her.)*

12. What does Mrs. Whatsit say that disturbs Mrs. Murry? *(Page 21, Mrs. Whatsit says, "…there is such a thing as a tesseract.")* How does Mrs. Murry show that she is shocked and alarmed? *(Page 21, Mrs. Murry turns white and clutches at a chair for support.)*

Prediction:
What does *tesseract* mean and who is Mrs. Whatsit?

Literary Analysis: Point of View
Point of view refers to the vantage point from which the narrator views the action of the story and relates it to the reader. In a first-person narrative, the story is told from the viewpoint of one person, usually the main character. A third-person omniscient narrator can "see over" everything that is happening and into each character's heart and mind. A third-person limited point of view means there are some restrictions on what can be seen; the narrator may know only what is happening to a few characters in one setting.

Ask: From what point of view does L'Engle tell the story in *A Wrinkle in Time*? How do you know?

Supplementary Activities:
Writing Activities:

1. Make a Venn diagram to compare your mother and Mrs. Murry, or your brother to Charles Wallace. Using a Venn diagram, develop the comparison in a paragraph.

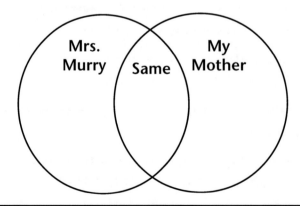

2. Meg describes the storm. How do you feel in a storm? Describe a storm that frightened you. Where were you? If you were in a house, what sounds did you hear? Could you see anything? How did you feel? Were you in danger? How long did the storm last? How did you handle your feelings?

Attribute Webs:

1. Begin webs for each of the characters. Work in small groups. Display and compare the webs. See pages 11-12 of this guide.

2. Draw a picture of the Murrys' house that captures the storm and the mystery of the night.

3. Meg has many feelings of insecurity. What is the dictionary definition of *insecurity*? What kind of situations promote insecurity? What are your feelings when insecure? Are there certain times of life that are filled with more insecurities? What are the best ways to handle insecurities? Brainstorm. Write five paragraphs using the organization and ideas from your brainstorming.

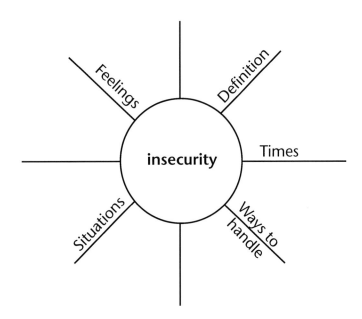

Chapter 2: "Mrs. Who"—Pages 22-37

Vocabulary:

unceremoniously 23	piteous 23	avid 26	ferocious 26
belligerent 26	antagonistic 27	tractable 27	sagely 29
inadvertently 30	indignation 31	disillusion 32	sport 32
compulsion 32	peremptory 36	assimilate 37	

Discussion Questions and Activities:

1. What do you think Mrs. Murry means when she says, "…you don't have to understand things for them to *be*"? *(page 23)* Give some examples.

2. How long has Mr. Murry been gone? *(Page 26, "…it was almost a year now since the last letter…")*

3. What do you think the principal means when he says, "…you'd make a better adjustment to life if you faced facts"? *(Page 26, The principal thinks that Mr. Murry has abandoned his family.)*

4. Why does Charles Wallace want to go see Mrs. Whatsit again? *(page 28, to find out more about the tesseract, to warn her and to tell her to be more careful)*

5. Why do people think Charles Wallace is strange? *(Page 24, He's odd and does not act like a little boy when he's around people other than the family. Pages 29-30, He knows what Meg and his mother are thinking even when they are not around.)* How is Charles' vocabulary different from the preschoolers you know? How does he learn such big words? *(Page 11, He tries to learn a big word every day.)*

6. Do you believe in ESP (Extrasensory Perception) or mental telepathy? How does Charles say he does it? *(Page 30, "…I just concentrate on you and Mother.")*

7. How are Charles Wallace and Calvin O'Keefe alike? *(Page 32, Calvin and Charles are sports.)* How does Charles define a *sport*? *(Page 32, "A change in gene resulting in the appearance in the offspring of a character which is not present in the parents but which is potentially transmissible to its offspring.")* What do you think this means? *(The two boys are very bright and very different from their parents.)*

8. Why does Calvin go for a walk to the haunted house? *(Page 33, "When I get this feeling, this compulsion, I always do what it tells me.")*

9. Why does Mrs. Who take the sheets? *(Pages 35-36, In case they need ghosts to frighten people away from the haunted house.)*

Prediction:
Who are these strange women? How are Charles, Calvin, and Meg going to work with them? Who is the good man that needs their help?

Literary Analysis: Characterization
Characterization is the way an author informs readers about what characters are like. Direct characterization is when the author describes the character. Indirect characterization is when the reader figures out what the character is like based on what the character thinks, says, or does.

Ask: What words and phrases would you use to describe Mrs. Who? *(Page 35, She is a plump little woman, who wears enormous spectacles, is sewing, and speaks in foreign languages using quotations from famous people.)* Of indirect characterization? *(page 36, thoughtful, grandmother-like)*

Characters' Motivation—A character's actions often tell you something about the character's thoughts and feelings. Watch each of the characters and try to determine why they do what they do.

Supplementary Activities:
1. Develop a cause-effect graphic organizer for one of the following situations:
   a) Meg has a fight with the boys coming home from school.
   b) Mrs. Whatsit drops in at the Murry house.
   c) Mrs. Buncombe loses her sheets.
   d) Mr. Murry leaves home.

2. Art: Some characters in this book are most unusual. Find descriptions of Mrs. Whatsit and Mrs. Who. Choose one of the characters. Make a realistic or an abstract picture showing how you think the character looks, showing something about the personality of the character as well as the physical characteristics or dress.

3. Writing: What did Mrs. Who tell Mrs. Whatsit about the children's visit? Write a short dialogue between Mrs. Who and Mrs. Whatsit. What do they think of the children? How do they propose to help them find their father?

Chapter 3: "Mrs. Which"—Pages 38-55

Prediction:
Chapter 3 is titled "Mrs. Which." What kind of character do you expect?

Vocabulary:

gamboled 38	megaparsec 43	essence 47	dubiously 47
dappled 49	morass 49	wafted 54	

Discussion Questions and Activities:
1. Calvin compares his mother to Mrs. Murry. Use a T-comparison chart to record class responses. (pages 12-13, 39-40)

Mrs. Murry	Mrs. O'Keefe
beautiful	upper teeth out
red hair, creamy skin	doesn't comb her hair
violet eyes	doesn't give a hoot about Calvin
loves her children	

2. Meg has some problems with schoolwork. Why? (*Pages 42-44, Meg and her father played math games and she learned too many shortcuts. Her handwriting is not legible and she's a little one-sided, but very bright. The teachers do not seem to like her or her attitude.*)

3. What mistake is there on page 44? What is the capital of New York state? (*Albany*)

4. What worries Mrs. Murry? (*Pages 45-46, She misses Mr. Murry and she is trying to find an explanation for his absence. She believes Mrs. Whatsit has part of the answer.*)

5. What rumor has Calvin heard about Mr. Murry? (*Page 49, He left his wife and family and went off with "some dame."*) How does Calvin calm Meg down when she reacts to his statement about Mr. Murry?

6. What was Mr. Murry doing when he disappeared? (*page 50, top secret government work*) What other kind of scientific work had he been involved with? (*Page 40, He had his picture taken with other scientists at Cape Canaveral, so he must have worked on space projects.*)

7. Why doesn't Mr. Murry communicate with his family? (*Page 52, They do not know but they know he is on a secret, dangerous mission.*)

8. Why have Mrs. Who, Mrs. Whatsit, and Mrs. Which come for the children? (*Page 53, Charles Wallace says, "…I think it's to find Father."*)

Prediction:
Where do you think Mr. Murry could be? What do you think Mrs. Who means when she says, "…wee hhave mmuch ttoo ddoo"? (page 55)

Literary Analysis: Imagery
Imagery is the use of sensory details—sounds, scents, tastes, textures, and especially sights. Point out the description of Mrs. Whatsit, Mrs. Who, and Mrs. Which. (pages 54-55) What does the author accomplish by using these sensory details?

Supplementary Activities:
1. Mrs. Who likes to quote. Keep a list of her quotations. Write your explanation of each quote.

2. There are no pictures in this book. What picture or symbol would you use for each chapter?

3. Create a bulletin board display depicting the characters in the novels and the setting.

Chapter 4: "The Black Thing"—Pages 56-73

Vocabulary:

corporeal 57	tangible 57	elliptic 58	ineffable 59
ephemeral 61	muted 64	flanks 64	exaltation 64
centaur 64	metamorphose 65	infinity 66	monoliths 66
resonant 67	incomprehensible 68	obscure 71	

Discussion Questions and Activities:

1. Describe Mrs. Which. How does she differ from Mrs. Who and Mrs. Whatsit? Use a triple Venn to point out how these characters are different and what they have in common. Add other characteristics as the novel is read.

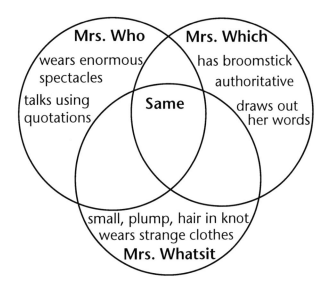

2. Why does Mrs. Who use quotations? *(Pages 60-61, She finds it difficult to verbalize. "It helps her if she can quote instead of working out words of her own.")*

3. Why do Mrs. Who, Mrs. Whatsit, and Mrs. Which take the children on a trip? *(pages 61-62, to find Father)*

4. What element of fantasy enables Meg, Charles, and Calvin to enter a different world? *(Page 62, "We tesser. Or you might say, we wrinkle.")*

5. How does the children's strange friend Mrs. Whatsit change or metamorphose? *(Page 64, She changes into something like a beautiful horse or centaur with a man's torso and wings.)* How does she carry the children? *(Page 65, They climb on her back and she flies off.)* What are the magic flowers used for? *(Page 70, When the atmosphere becomes thin, they breathe through the flower and they get just enough oxygen.)*

---

6. How would you describe the "Black Thing"? *(Page 72, It is a shadow so terrible that it blots out the light of the stars. It fills Meg "with a fear that is beyond shuddering, beyond crying or screaming...")*

Prediction:
Why do you think the children have been shown the "Black Thing"?

Literary Analysis: Mood
When one feeling in a story is stronger than the other, that feeling is called the mood of the story. What is the mood at the end of Chapter 4? How does the author's description of the Black Thing create that mood? How did you feel as you read this chapter? What feelings would the characters in this novel experience in this chapter?

Supplementary Activity:
Draw and color an abstract shape that reflects the mood of the chapter. Also write a paragraph summarizing the chapter and describing how your drawing reflects the mood.

Chapter 5: "The Tesseract"—Pages 74-90

Vocabulary:

illuminating 78	dissolution 79	intolerable 80	materialize 81
substantial 81	protoplasm 81	transition 84	reverberated 86

Discussion Questions and Activities:
1. How does Mrs. Whatsit explain *tessering*? What visuals does the author use to help the reader? What examples does Mrs. Whatsit use? Would paper and pencil have helped Mrs. Whatsit's explanation? *(Pages 76-78, Tessering is traveling through space without having to go the long way around. The author uses a straight line, a square, a cube, and examples from math to help the children understand.)*

2. What mistake does Mrs. Which make when she "tessers" the children? *(Pages 79-80, She tessers them briefly to a two-dimensional planet where the three-dimensional children experience intolerable pressure.)*

3. Why do the children stop on the belt of Orion? *(page 81, to have a look at planet earth and to meet a friend of Mrs. Who, Mrs. Which, and Mrs. Whatsit)*

4. Why isn't Mrs. Murry going to be worried about the children being gone? *(Page 82, They take a time wrinkle as well as a space wrinkle. They will be back about five minutes before they left.)*

5. Why is the Happy Medium's name a good one? *(Page 83, She's very jolly and laughs and assures Mrs. Whatsit that everything is going to come out right as*

long as she can laugh.) What does the Happy Medium show the children? *(Pages 86-87, She shows them the Dark Thing on earth.)*

6. Why does Mrs. Whatsit show the children the Dark Thing on Uriel? *(Pages 87-88, "...because the atmosphere on the mountain peaks there is so clear and thin you could see it for what it is. And we thought it would be easier for you understand it if you saw it—well, someplace else first, not your own earth.")*

7. Why does Mrs. Whatsit say the planet earth is troubled? *(pages 87-88, the Dark Thing, Evil—the Powers of Darkness)* Brainstorm the word EVIL. Let students suggest all the things or people who are evil. What does the Black Thing mean to you? Develop a word map for EVIL. Use color to distinguish antonyms, synonyms, etc.

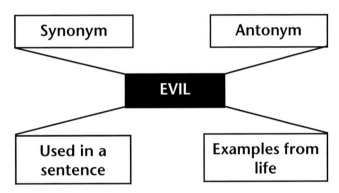

8. Who has fought the Evil Powers? *(page 89, Jesus, artists, scientists, great people of earth)* How did they fight the Evil Powers?

Prediction:
What does the Happy Medium see in her great ball? Why is she crying?

Literary Analysis: Plot
Plot is the action in the story. Usually a plot progresses through four stages—exposition, rising action, climax, and resolution or falling action. Place these stages on a large sheet of paper. Review the chapters read. Add incidents for each stage as the chapters are completed. This is another form of the story map.

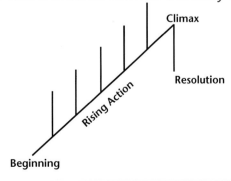

Supplementary Activities:
1. Draw a picture of what the Happy Medium sees in her great ball.

2. Collect newspaper stories about evil in today's world.

Chapter 6: "The Happy Medium"—Pages 91-113

Vocabulary:

anticlimax 93	facet 93	ambrosia 94	nectar 94
eon 98	malignant 99	precipitously 99	sumac 99
propitious 100	talisman 100	simultaneously 103	furtive 104
aberration 106			

Discussion Questions and Activities:
1. What had Mrs. Whatsit been? *(page 92, a star)* How and why did she give up her life as a star? *(page 92, in battle with the Thing)*

2. What does Mrs. Whatsit give each of the children so they can deal with the problems of Camazotz? *(pages 100-101, Calvin—the ability to communicate; Meg—her faults; Charles Wallace—the resilience of childhood)* What does Mrs. Whatsit call these presents to the children? *(page 100, talismans)* What does Mrs. Who give to the children? *(Page 101, She tells Charles to remember he doesn't know everything and she gives her glasses to Meg.)* What special instructions does Mrs. Which give the children before they go into the town? *(Page 101, Mrs. Which tells them to stay together and not let anybody or thing separate them.)* Is this a sign of their great danger? Why is there more danger for Charles Wallace? *(Page 102, He is "by far the most vulnerable.")*

3. What do the children first see when they arrive in Camazotz? *(pages 99-100, a town that does not look strange at first—just boring)* How are the people of Camazotz unusual? *(pages 103-104)* Who do the children talk to? What do they learn? How does the paperboy differ from the housewife and the little boy? *(pages 104-109)*

4. Would you like to live in Camazotz? Why or why not?

5. What do the children learn about CENTRAL Central Intelligence? *(page 108)* Who do you think IT is?

6. How did you feel when you read this chapter? How did the author create the mood or atmosphere? What words helped create the mood? Was there fear, suspense, or other feelings there?

Prediction:
On page 113, Calvin says, "...if we go into that building [CENTRAL Central Intelligence] we're going into terrible danger." What do you think will happen?

Literary Analysis: Figurative Language
A *metaphor* is a comparison between two things, without the words "like" or "as." A *simile* is a comparison using the words "like" or "as." *Personification* is giving human characteristics to an animal or an object.

How would you classify these quotations?

* page 3,   "Behind the trees clouds scudded frantically across the sky."
* page 64,   "...something like a horse..."
* page 65,   "...and the radiance of the smile was as tangible as a soft breeze..."
* page 91,   "The earth with its fearful covering of dark shadow swam out of view..."

Supplementary Activities:
1. Character Chart: Make a large character chart. Add characters as we meet them in the novel. For each of the characters describe when they experience the feelings listed. See the next page of this guide.

2. Students will select a character and a passage that best illustrates what the character is feeling. Students will expand the dialogue into a character monologue.

Chapter 7: "The Man With Red Eyes"—Pages 114-132

Vocabulary:

bilious 115	unsubstantial 115	procedure 116	arrogance 117
bravado 117	requisition 118	recourse 121	impressionable 123
obliquely 123	diverting 127	synthetic 127	tenacity 128
indecisively 129	belligerent 132		

Discussion Questions and Activities:
1. How did you feel as you read about the children going into the CENTRAL Central Intelligence building? *(page 115)*

2. How does Charles Wallace play with words when he says, "Strawberry jam or raspberry?" *(Page 117, The odd gentleman said, "I am here to report that one of my letters is jamming..." Charles uses another meaning of jam.)*

3. What do you think Meg means when she wonders about Charles's arrogance as a cover or bravado? *(page 117)* What danger does Mrs. Whatsit point out to Charles? *(Page 117, He has to watch being proud.)*

Character Chart

Feeling	Meg	Charles Wallace	Mr. Murry	Mrs. Whatsit
Frustration				
Anger				
Fear				
Humiliation				
Relief				

4. How does the man with red eyes communicate with the children? *(Page 120, "...he had somehow communicated directly into their brains.")*

5. How does the man with red eyes try to gain control of Charles? *(pages 121, 126, by hypnotism)* How does Charles keep the man from hypnotizing the others? *(page 122, by reciting nursery rhymes)*

6. How does Meg try to save Charles? *(Page 126, She runs after him and tackles him, and cracks his head on the floor.)*

7. Why does the food taste like sand to Charles and not to Calvin and Meg? *(Page 130, Charles has shut his mind to the man. Calvin and Meg can't completely close their minds.)*

8. Why does Charles Wallace finally go in to the man with red eyes? *(page 130, to find out about him, find out what he really is and to find out where Father is)*

Prediction:
Will Charles Wallace be able to escape? How will Meg and Calvin rescue him?

Literary Analysis: Suspense and Conflict
Suspense is the tension and uncertainty about what will happen next. What words help create suspense? Why do you think the author uses suspense?

Supplementary Activity:
Nature of Conflict: Conflict is the struggle or clash between two opposing forces, one of which is usually a person, often the main character, called the protagonist. Conflict occurs when the protagonist struggles against an antagonist or opposing force. The excitement in novels develops from the use of conflict.

Kinds: There are four main types of conflict.

1. Person-against-person
2. Person against-nature
3. Person-against-society
4. Person-against-self

Who is the antagonist in *A Wrinkle in Time?* Who is the protagonist in *A Wrinkle in Time?* See the next page of this guide.

Below list some of the conflicts from the novel. In the space provided, briefly describe the conflict and indicate which type of conflict is involved, writing the number from the previous page.

Conflict	Description	Type

Conflict #1 resolution: _____

Conflict #2 resolution: _____

Conflict #3 resolution: _____

Chapter 8: "The Transparent Column"—Pages 133-143

Vocabulary:

infuriated 134	bland 135	spindly 135	pinioned 135
primitive 136	swivet 138	marionette 138	misconception 139
pedantic 139	annihilate 139	sadist 141	monotonous 142
emanate 143	deviate 143		

Discussion Questions and Activities:
1. Prove that Charles Wallace has been taken over, hypnotized, or possessed by the man with red eyes.

   • page 133—Charles ate the turkey that tasted like sand as if it were delicious.
   • page 133—His eyes were different. The little boy in his place was only a copy.
   • page 134—Charles Wallace says Mrs. Whatsit, Mrs. Who and Mrs. Which are really the enemy.
   • page 136—He says, "Relax and be happy."

2. How has Camazotz conquered all illness and deformity? *(Page 139, Anyone who gets sick or deviates is "put to sleep.")* How is this like Nazi Germany?

3. Charles Wallace says, "Differences create problems." (page 140) Ask students to brainstorm all the problems created by differences. The teacher will list the problems. The class will list possible solutions for the problems.

4. Discuss the meanings of IT. *(Page 141, Charles Wallace calls IT the Boss.)* What happens when people resist the power of IT? What happens to the boy who doesn't bounce his ball in rhythm? *(Page 143, When there is lack of cooperation, IT takes care to retrain. Each time the little boy bounces the ball he screams.)*

Prediction:
Charles leads the others to Father who is imprisoned in a transparent column. If you were Meg and Calvin, what would you do to get him out? Teacher writes predictions on a chart.

What do you think IT will look like? Teacher lists students' responses.

Literary Analysis: Dialogue
Dialogue is the conversation in a story or play. The exact words a person says are quoted; quotation marks point out the dialogue. See Supplementary Activity #1 below.

Supplementary Activities:
1. Choose a section of dialogue. Complete the dialogue activity on page 28 of this guide.

2. Research Nazi Germany's elimination of the handicapped and mentally ill as well as the Jews and people with political differences.

Chapter 9: "IT"—Pages 144-162

Vocabulary:

placidly 146	menacing 149	gibberish 150	myopic 153
insolent 153	angular 156	ominous 156	inexorable 157
dais 157	disembodied 158	nauseating 158	systole 159
diastole 159	miasma 159		

Discussions Questions and Activities:
1. Where does Meg find her father? How has he changed? *(Pages 144-145, Mr. Murry is imprisoned in the transparent column. He has grown a beard and his hair is very long.)*

2. How does Meg free her father? *(Pages 148-149, She uses the spectacles from Mrs. Who which allow her to walk through the column.)*

Using Dialogue

Directions: Choose a bit of dialogue from the book to investigate. Fill in the chart to describe this way of writing and telling a story.

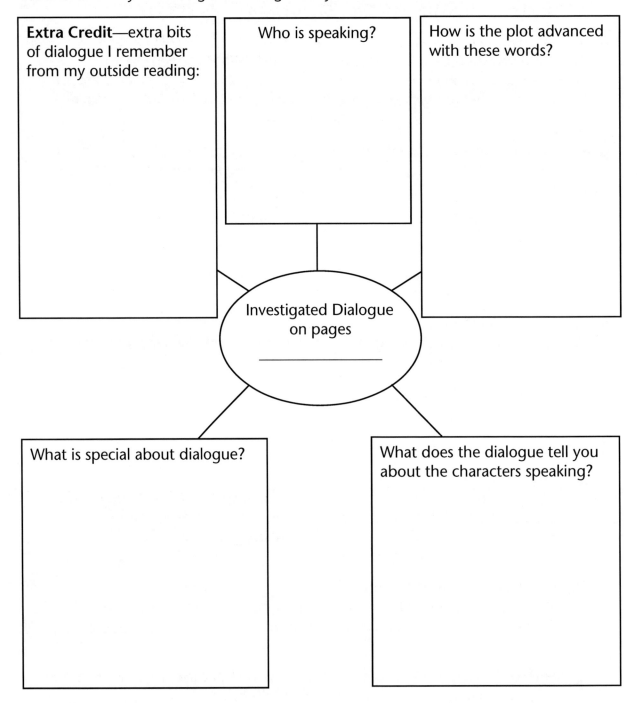

Extra Credit—extra bits of dialogue I remember from my outside reading:

Who is speaking?

How is the plot advanced with these words?

Investigated Dialogue on pages

_____

What is special about dialogue?

What does the dialogue tell you about the characters speaking?

3. How are the walls on Camazotz different from those on earth? *(Page 151, One can rearrange the atoms of a wall and walk through it. Mrs. Who's glasses help the atoms rearrange.)*

4. How do Meg and her father get out of the column? *(Page 152, Meg wraps her arms around her father who has Mrs. Who's spectacles on his nose and they pass through the column.)*

5. How does Meg answer Charles Wallace's statement, "…that's exactly what we have on Camazotz. Complete equality. Everybody exactly alike"? *(Page 160, Meg said, "Like and equal are not the same thing at all!")* What would you say?

6. How does Meg avoid being taken over by IT? *(Page 162, She tessers with her father.)*

Prediction:
Do you think Meg will survive? This is only Chapter 9, so what could happen in the rest of this book?

Literary Analysis: Style
Just as people have certain hair styles or clothing styles, authors have particular styles of writing. An author's style depends on the words he or she uses and the types of sentences he or she writes. Some authors use a lot of words that appeal to the senses or have many long, flowery sentences. Others write in short sentences or use simple "spare" prose. How would you describe the author's writing style in *A Wrinkle in Time*?

Supplementary Activities:
1. Review Meg's actions, thoughts, etc. Reread parts of the story. Jot down phrases and page references in the boxes on the chart on the next page of this guide. For each group of details, write a generalization about Meg. Then summarize your generalizations in one or two sentences.

2. Drama: Divide the class into groups. Find scenes that the groups may reenact.

Character Review

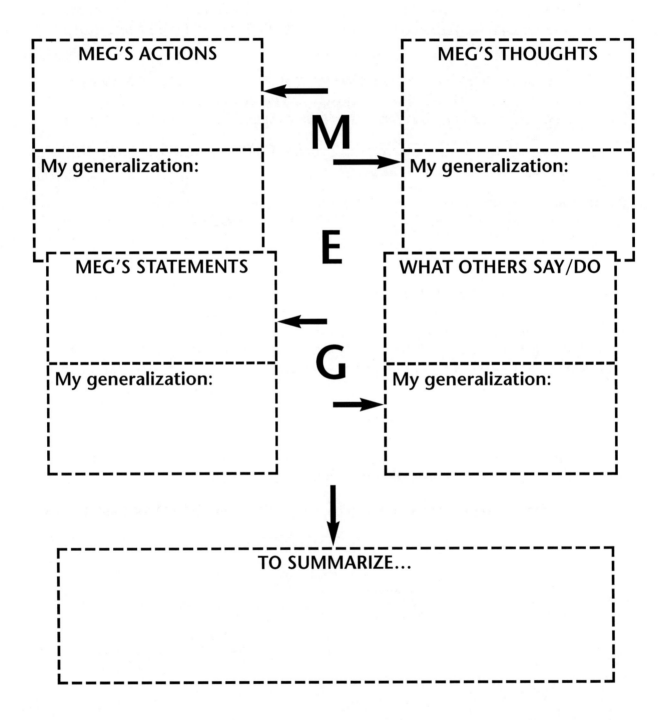

MEG'S ACTIONS

My generalization:

M

MEG'S THOUGHTS

My generalization:

E

MEG'S STATEMENTS

My generalization:

G

WHAT OTHERS SAY/DO

My generalization:

TO SUMMARIZE...

Chapter 10: "Absolute Zero"—Pages 163-175

Vocabulary:

atrophied 164	disintegration 167	corrosive 171	omnipotent 172
fallible 172	tentacles 173	indentations 173	

Discussion Questions and Activities:

1. How is Mr. Murry able to get Calvin and Meg away from IT? *(Page 164, "Because IT's completely unused to being refused...No mind has tried to hold out against IT for so many thousands of centuries that certain centers have become soft and atrophied through lack of use.")*

2. Why did Mr. Murry go to Camazotz? *(Page 165, It was an accident. He was tessering to Mars.)*

3. How is IT able to get Charles Wallace before Meg and Calvin? *(Page 165, "He trusted too much to his own strength...")*

4. Where are Meg, Calvin, and Mr. Murry after they tesser? *(Page 170, They do not know.)*

5. How does Meg act after her father and Calvin tesser out of Camazotz? *(Page 172, She is very cold, her heart is barely beating and she is as much in the power of the Black Thing as Charles Wallace.)*

6. How do the strange creatures in this place differ from the creatures on Uriel and Camazotz? *(Page 173, They seem like animals except they walk upright.)*

Prediction:

Three strange creatures with four arms, tentacles, and queer faces pick up Meg and take her on the last page of Chapter 10. Where will they take her? What adventures will she have now?

Literary Analysis: Cause/Effect

When examining the reason for events in a story, we often find that: a) one cause has several results, or b) several causes lead to the same result.

Supplementary Activity:

Think about the various effects in *A Wrinkle in Time*. Organize the chain of events and determine what sets things off (the cause). Use the following diagrams to explain to your classmates cause and effect.

Cause/Effect Chart

Directions: When examining the reason for events in a story, we often find that:

    a) one cause has several results, or
    b) several causes lead to the same result.

    1. Think about the various effects the kidnapping has on the family. Organize the chain of events it sets off within the map below.

How do Mr. Murry's actions affect the rest of his family?

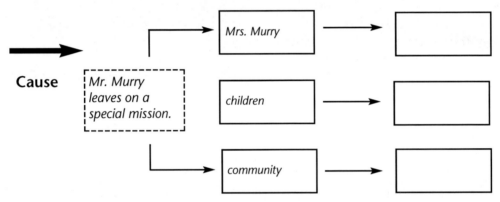

    2. Organize some of these reasons (causes of actions) within the map below.

Why do Charles Wallace and Meg tesseract?

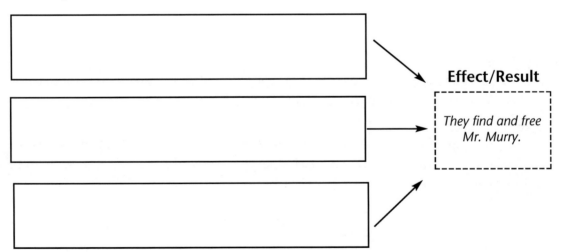

Cause/Effect Chart

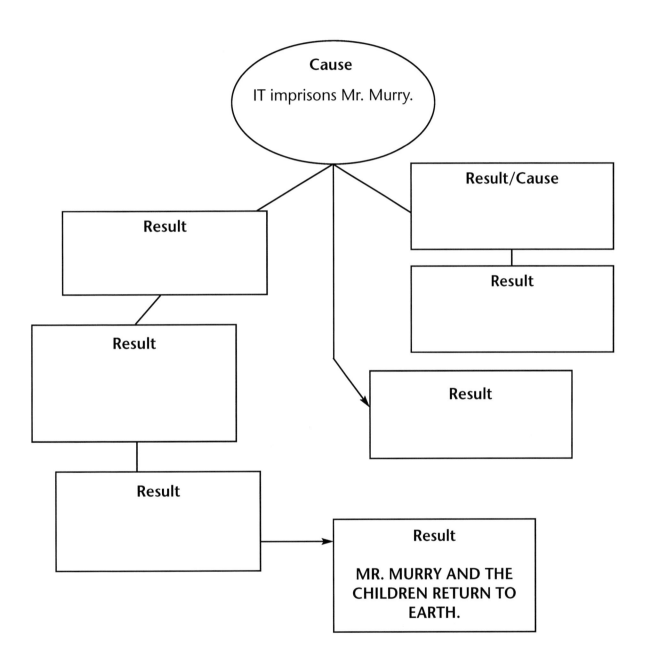

Cause

IT imprisons Mr. Murry.

Result

Result/Cause

Result

Result

Result

Result

Result

MR. MURRY AND THE CHILDREN RETURN TO EARTH.

Chapter 11: "Aunt Beast"—Pages 176-191

Vocabulary:

emanate 176	tremor 177	trepidation 177	acute 178
counteracted 179	pungent 180	relinquish 180	perplexity 181
opaque 181	jeopardize 183	vulnerable 183	converged 187
despondency 188	distraught 189	reverberated 191	

Discussion Questions and Activities:

1. Why do the beasts think that it is a limiting thing to have the ability to see? *(Page 181, They have no eyes; they know what things are, not what they look like.)*

2. How do the beasts help Meg? *(Pages 180-185, Aunt Beast feeds her, gives her a warm fur, and sings her to sleep.)*

3. Why is Aunt Beast the strangest creature in this novel?

4. Is Aunt Beast's appearance consistent with her behavior?

5. What problem do Meg and the others face? *(Page 188, Someone must go back to Camazotz for Charles Wallace.)*

6. How does Meg try to describe Mrs. Whatsit, Mrs. Who, and Mrs. Which? What do you think Aunt Beast means when she says, "Think about what they *are*. This *look* doesn't help us at all"? *(page 190)*

Prediction:
The last sentence in Chapter 11 is "WWEEE ARRE HHERRE!" Who could this be? How will this book end?

Literary Analysis: Climax
Climax is the moment in a novel or play at which a crisis comes to its point of greatest intensity and is in some manner resolved.

Supplementary Activities:

1. Write five words to describe Aunt Beast. Why is she strange? Is she a good creature? How do you know?

2. Review the chapters of this novel. For Meg, provide a phrase describing her emotions in each chapter. Complete the chart on page 35 of this guide. For example, in Chapter 1, Meg is frightened and depressed.

Feelings

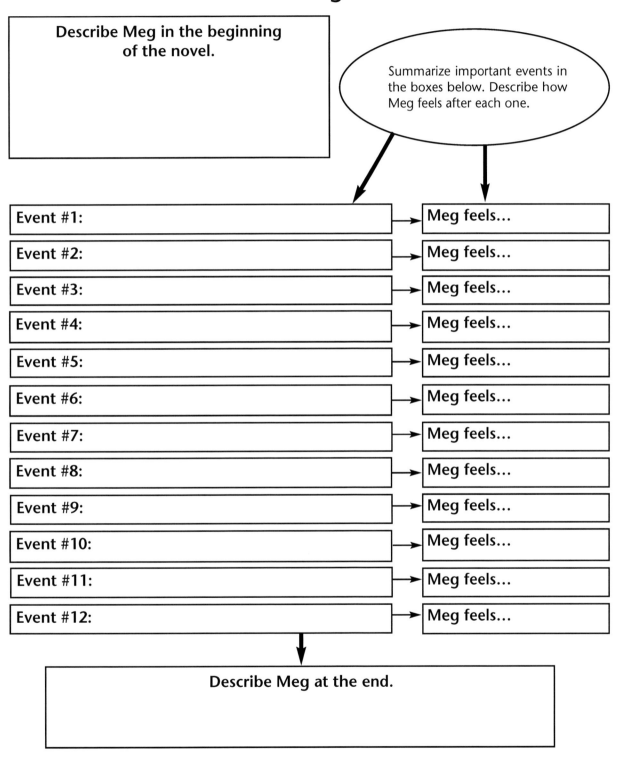

Describe Meg in the beginning of the novel.

Summarize important events in the boxes below. Describe how Meg feels after each one.

Event #1: | Meg feels...

Event #2: | Meg feels...

Event #3: | Meg feels...

Event #4: | Meg feels...

Event #5: | Meg feels...

Event #6: | Meg feels...

Event #7: | Meg feels...

Event #8: | Meg feels...

Event #9: | Meg feels...

Event #10: | Meg feels...

Event #11: | Meg feels...

Event #12: | Meg feels...

Describe Meg at the end.

Chapter 12: "The Foolish and the Weak"—Pages 192-211

Vocabulary:

appallingly 193	formidably 195	ministrations 195	imperceptibly 204
permeating 205	inexorable 205	reiterating 206	unadulterated 207
animated 208	catapulted 210		

Discussion Questions and Activities:

1. What does Mrs. Whatsit mean when she says, "We want nothing from you that you do without grace or that you do without understanding"? Has anyone ever said something like that to you? *(page 195)*

2. Why does it have to be Meg who will attempt to rescue Charles Wallace? *(Pages 195-196, Charles understands her. She is the one who is closest to him.)*

3. Mrs. Whatsit compares life to a sonnet. "You're given the form, but you have to write the sonnet yourself. What you say is completely up to you." What do you think this means? *(page 199)*

4. What gift does Mrs. Whatsit give Meg before she returns to Camazotz? *(page 201, her love)*

5. When Meg returns to Camazotz she has a weapon from Mrs. Which but she does not know what it is. *(page 203)* Do you know how she overcomes IT? *(Page 207, "She could love Charles Wallace.")*

6. How has Meg changed Camazotz and how has Camazotz changed her?

Post-reading Questions

1. Do you think the conclusion of this novel was realistic? Could you improve this ending? How?

2. Do you think the author revealed her personal attitudes? biases? What were they?

3. Summarize the story using a story diagram like the one below.

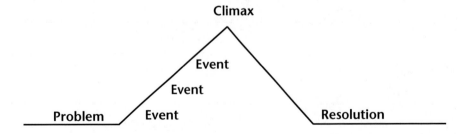

4. Characterization: Characters are developed by what they say, think, and do and by how others in the novel react to them. Which characters in the novel provided wisdom and perspective? Can you identify any characters who protested against injustice and inequities in this story? Who are they? How did they protest? Which character changed in this book? How would you explain the changes?

5. Is Meg a heroine? Why or why not?

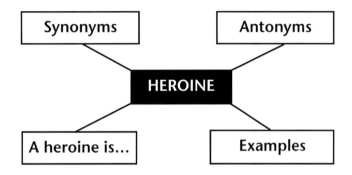

6. The setting (time and place) was more important in this story than it is in some others. Why? What different places were named? List each place and a short phrase to describe the place and the mood.

7. Plot: In literature the plot often is carried along by the causes and effects of decisions made by the main characters. Had a character made an alternate decision, the plot would have turned in a different direction. What were the important decisions or turning points of this story?

8. What was the saddest moment in the book? the happiest?

9. Theme is the novel's central idea. What is this author's message? Why do you think the author wrote this story? What do you think is the most important thing to remember about this story? Support your ideas for the theme or themes with examples from the novel. Is the central theme of this story presented directly or indirectly?

Post-reading Extension Activities

Creative Writing:
1. Imagine that you are a TV script writer and one of the networks has decided to create a series based on this novel. Write the outline for one episode (taken from the novel, or from your imagination). Include not only dialogue, but visual images you would like to capture on film.

2. You are a newspaper reporter. Write an account of one of the following: Mrs. Buncombe has lost her sheets, mysterious activities at the old haunted house, or a report of people tumbling out of the sky into a garden. Include a headline, what happened, who was involved, when, where, why, and some bystander quotes.

3. Write the dialogue between Mr. and Mrs. Murry after Mr. Murry returns home.

4. Describe Charles Wallace from the points of view of five people who know him: Meg, Mrs. Murry, the twins, and Calvin.

5. Rewrite the scene where Meg goes back to rescue Charles Wallace.

6. Respond to the novel by writing a poem.

7. Write a flashback scene to an earlier time that didn't appear in the novel, but might have—such as a scene showing Mr. Murry making the mistake that landed him on Camazotz and in the Transparent Column.

8. Come up with your own chapter titles for each chapter. (These titles often refer to a key episode in the chapter, a phrase found in the chapter, or a new character who appears in the chapter.)

Listening/Speaking/Drama:
1. Stage a TV interview with some of the central characters in the story. (Meg, Charles Wallace, Mrs. Who, Mrs. Whatsit, Mrs. Which, or Aunt Beast) For homework, students playing each role gather impressions about what their character is like. Other students make lists of interview questions. (e.g., "Meg— What did you have that IT did not have? How did you show that you had this quality?" "Charles Wallace, what bothered you the most when you were left behind with IT? Or did anything of the past good times remain with you?")

2. Retell an episode from the viewpoint of IT.

3. Present a scene from the novel in dramatic form.

4. Work with a partner to write an imaginary dialogue between yourself and one of the characters in the novel.

Language Study:
1. Characters in this novel are full of colorful expression. Make a list of your favorites, and put the meaning of each into your own words.

2. Mrs. Who had trouble verbalizing, so she used many quotations. Make a list of these quotations and tell what Mrs. Who is trying to say.

3. Make a list of examples of figurative language used in the story (metaphors, similes, personification.) Briefly analyze each one, telling what is being compared and why the comparison is effective.

4. There are several allusions in the story (e.g., da Vinci, Shakespeare, Bach, Pasteur, etc.). Make a list of other allusions, and find out the source and meaning of each.

Art:

1. Create a group mural showing important scenes from the novel.

2. Create a triptych (3 panels) showing your impressions of Meg—at school, at home, in the Transparent Column.

3. Create a mobile showing objects of significance to the story. (Attach the mobile to a hanger or to the straight side of half of a paper plate with thread.) For instance, you might include a pair of spectacles, sheets, broomstick, crystal ball, etc.

4. Create a shoebox diorama showing a memorable scene from the story—the Transparent Column, the children and Mr. Murry tumbling into the family garden, etc.

5. Some of the characters in this book are most unusual. Find descriptions of Mrs. Whatsit, Mrs. Who and Mrs. Which. Make a realistic or an abstract picture showing how you think the character and/or characters look showing something about the personality of the character as well as the physical characteristics or dress.

Music:

1. Find examples of music that could be used in the TV program based on the novel.

2. Write a ballad about the faithful love of Mrs. Murry during the lonely years of Mr. Murry's disappearance, and set it to the tune of a popular ballad such as "On Top of Old Smoky" or "Barbara Allen."

Science:

1. Find out more about the research procedures of Cape Canaveral. What backgrounds do these scientists have? Write for information about space exploration.

2. Make a list of physical characteristics of Camazotz and the belt of Orion.

Current Events:

Comb recent newspapers and magazine for articles, cartoons, etc. that somehow tie in with the novel. For instance, you might find an article about UFOs, an article about life on Mars, water on Mars, etc. Create a poster from the various clippings. In each case, write a sentence or two explaining the connection between the current piece and the novel.

Assessment for *A Wrinkle in Time*

Assessment is an ongoing process, more than a quiz at the end of the book. Points may be added by the teacher to show the level of achievement. When an item is completed, the teacher and the student check it.

Name _____ Date _____

Student   **Teacher**

_____   _____   1. Complete a story map for the novel. See page 10 of this guide.

_____   _____   2. Make an attribute web for Charles Wallace. See pages 11-12 of this guide.

_____   _____   3. Make a T-comparison chart showing the difference between realistic fiction and science fiction. Why is *A Wrinkle in Time* science fiction? Use specific examples from the novel. Put this on your chart.

_____   _____   4. Compare Charles Wallace to boys you know using a T-comparison chart for pre-writing a short comparison.

_____   _____   5. Complete a prediction chart like the one on page 9 of this guide. How many times were your predictions correct?

_____   _____   6. Keep a dialogue journal with one of the characters in the novel. Write questions you would like to ask the character about the character's feelings, reactions, beliefs, motives or actions.

_____   _____   7. Complete the Nature of Conflict Chart on page 26 of this guide.

_____   _____   8. Some of the characters in this book are most unusual. Find descriptions of Mrs. Whatsit, Mrs. Who, and Mrs. Which. Make a realistic or an abstract picture showing how you think the character and/or characters look showing something about the personality of the character as well as the physical characteristics or dress.

_____   _____   9. There are no pictures in the book. What picture or symbol would you use for each chapter?

_____   _____   10. Write a letter to a friend advising him/her to read or not read this novel. Give specific reasons.